MW01242475

"We the People" XXI

Twenty-First Century THINKING

About the author

Porter Davis is a visionary. He sees ideas that
will help people. Then he attracts professionals
who will be part of the team, to bring the
visions to life. He has a B.A in political science
and a real estate certificate from UC Berkeley,
attended Hastings Law School, and was an Area
Governor of Toastmasters. He had a
successful mortgage company and is a Financial
Coach and the founder of Pacific Rim Group.
He finds creative solutions and inspires people
to do things that they didn't think that they
could do. Porter is extremely passionate about
everything he takes on - from starting his own
shoe-shine business at the age of 7, to driving
5,500 miles around the country to 7 states,
advocating for Hillary's Presidential campaign
in 2016.

His passion, now, is in speaking to university
students about Voting and Democracy.
This led to a speaking tour in 2020.
**That tour, "WE THE PEOPLE",
continues.**

FOR MY LOVES

"I honor them for shaping my life"

Leslie, Shannon, Beverly, Melinda, Karen,
Sandra, Brigitte, Maritza

FOR MY BUDDIES

"Unconditional support"

Ted Craig, for 81 years.
Pat McAlonan, for 46 years.

FOR MY MOM

"GYP"
1900 B-Day - 1915 "Suffragette"

TABLE OF CONTENTS

PREFACE

We were awakened in 2020 about where the
POWER is, and how to preserve "it".
"It" is "us".

This book is about "us".
The Title "We the People" XXI
comes from the Preamble to the United States
Constitution:

"We the People of the United States, in order
to form a more perfect union, establish justice,
ensure domestic tranquility, provide for the
common defense, promote the general welfare,
and secure the Blessings of Liberty to ourselves
and our posterity, do ordain and establish this
Constitution for the United States of America".

And then I ask 3 questions
Who are "we"?
Who aren't "we"?
and
Why is it important?

In 1787 the Founders established a Democracy. In a Democracy the POWER is in the people. They get it by their "right to vote". I will discuss this "right" and how we can share it with all the people in the United States of America, in the twenty-first century.

Then I will make a case to RE-ORDAIN and RE-ESTABLISH the Constitution, using twenty-first century thinking.

****

INTRODUCTION

In 399BC, in Athens Greece, Socrates was
tried, convicted, and sentenced to death;

what for?

corrupting his students;

How?

ENCOURAGING THEM TO

THINK!

1. The Preamble to the U. S Constitution: Who were "THEY"?

In 1787 the Constitutional Convention adopted the United States Constitution.

In 1787 Gouvernuer Morris was given the task to come up with an introduction to the Constitution. So, what did he do? He came up with a Preamble. He said, We the people. He did not say; We the citizens. He did not say, We the white men, who are over the age of 21, and who own property. He truly was a "Visionary".

Why? Because he said "We the people" ----- do ordain and establish this Constitution for the United States of America.

The Preamble to the United States Constitution;

"We the people of the United states in order to form a more perfect union, establish justice, ensure domestic tranquility, provide for the common defense, promote the general welfare, and secure the blessings of liberty to ourselves and our posterity, do ordain and establish this Constitution for the United States of America."

There were only thirteen states at the time, with a population of 4,000,000. Of those 4,000,000 it was only white men, over the age of 21 and property owners, who really ordained and established our Constitution. It was estimated that they constituted about 6% of the population, or about 240,000 people.

Therefore "WE" did not "ORDAIN" and "ESTABLISH" this constitution.

"THEY" did!

If you were part of the other 3,000,000+ who were not included, do you think you would feel left out?

AND

What kind of a culture did it establish?

2. My History

My Mom was born in 1900 and was a suffragette [supporters of women's right to vote]. In 1915 she walked down 5th Ave in New York with 25,000 other women protesting the Founding Fathers' THINKING, which left out women. It took 132 years for women to get the right to vote. And slowly all the other groups that were left out started to protest against that THINKING..

[That kind of THINKING still goes on today, in 2020].

In 1933 I was born.
In 1953 I was a Korean War Vet.
In 1958 I graduated from University of California at Berkeley.
In 1962 I was the father of 4 children and finished law school.
In 1964 I was a coordinator for a Presidential campaign.
In 1968 I was chairman for an Assembly campaign.

I have spoken to large and small groups over the last 50 years. One of my signature speeches is called: "Conversation, Cookies and Coffee". Audiences are often excited by my dynamic charismatic delivery.

I have been a trainer for Dale Carnegie Courses, an Area Governor for Toastmasters, an assistant in the Speaking Freely courses, an affiliate member of the Northern California Chapter of The National Speakers Association, a candidate for local office, a coordinator for 47 Northern California counties in the 1964 presidential campaign, chairman of an assembly campaign and promoter for the 2016 Hillary presidential campaign.

I was a candidate for governor of Boys State, a graduate of the University of California at Berkeley, with a Bachelor of Arts Degree in Political Science, finished Hastings Law School, a father, grandfather, and a Korean War Veteran.

I have a passion to bring about Social change in the 21st century, using the electronic systems available. These are my 9 + 1 favorite Social Causes:

1-Citizenville
2- C to C Health Care
3- The Golden Gate Bridge
4- Delancey City
5- The HOPEprogram
6- Right to Die
7- Lifetime Education
8- Red Carpet Immigration
9- The Electric Challenge
+1- Bill of "Human Rights"

1-**Citizenville:**

Citizenville is California Governor Gavin Newsom's book on the changes that will and are occurring in our society in the 21st century. He notes that government has become bogged down in politics and is failing to do their job, thus, opening up opportunities for the people to band together in small groups and take on the needed tasks that will be beneficial to all of us.

2-**C to C Health Care:**

Health care [from CONCEPTION TO CELEBRATION OF LIFE] is a basic "Human Right" for all the people and includes all residents in the United States [WHICH WE WILL LATER CALL GLOBAL CITIZENS]. It will be run by a member of the medical profession as a Secretary of Health.

It will have the same health care as Congress votes for themselves, and the same facilities. It will include vision, mental, dental, and all proven alternative health systems that are unfolding worldwide.

Upgrading all facilities will create more jobs and income and the resultant taxes, thus more than paying for the program. An important outfall from this way of thinking will be to develop part of a healing process as we no longer exclude anyone, or any needed health care.

We are developing our thinking to include everyone, and it will give us the chance to live up to the vision of Gouveneur Morris in the Preamble: "We the people".

The facilities will be built in every community nation-wide. This program will pay for itself. Also, and more importantly, it will create a new feeling of togetherness, never attained in peace times. This program, the jobs, and the psychological impact on everyone in our country, because of the common cause, it will create a new society.

If we compare it with the present society where we build a high-tech aircraft carrier, send it to waters in and near many other countries, and see what it does to the framework of our society. It shows strength to our friends and a threat to our enemies. Also, it eats at our subconscious and we create "ill will" around the world, and within ourselves.

The cost of developing, training, building, operating, and maintaining the Aircraft Carrier would pay for health care for everyone in the United States for more than 2 years.

It would eliminate the need for insurance companies. Now, you take the two concepts and compare them. You will see that one is defensive and based on power, greed and fear, while the other one is based on sharing and caring for one another.

When a society decides to take on a task that looks impossible and succeeds there is a wonderful feeling of accomplishment for the common good.

For Example: WWII, The Voyager space shuttles, the US highway system, John Kennedy's challenge to have a man on the moon by the end of the decade. There are many more. We must start from the ground, and that is our Democracy, it is to include everyone.

3-The Golden Gate Bridge:

We have been given this "International Icon" as a great connector of our Northern California communities. But what we really have is this magnificent structure that seemed to the average person, and many civil engineering experts, impossible to build over the Golden Gate waters between Marin County and San Francisco, in the 1920-30's.

The treacherous waters, the howling winds, and the depth of the channel, more than 200 feet in places, made the construction a major feat. As residents of the San Francisco Bay Area, we have the opportunity and the obligation to protect and preserve it.

The growing population, the burgeoning economy, the need for education and for transportation have magnified the costs to maintain the bridge. We have addressed this by developing a system wide bus system. We have expanded the ferry system. And we have set in motion the Golden Gate Bridge Highway and Transportation District to oversee them. In order, to maintain and develop these entities, maintenance of the bridge has been cut back.

Taking Newsom's lead, I started "The Golden Gate Bridge Beautification Foundation" (TGGBBF). Its purpose is to take care of the maintenance costs of the Bridge, develop a major parking facility, revamp the museum, and update the administration building, including 20 to 40 story mixed use housing...

Funding for the program will come from major fund-raising events and activities for everyone of all ages, and lovers of the Bridge, worldwide.

I remember driving across her in 1938 and looking at the mighty structure. I fell in love at first sight. And I have never failed to keep my commitment of love.

When I graduated from Alameda High school, in 1951, I took a summer job working on the bridge. It was the toughest work I have ever done, but when I love something there is nothing that can deter me.

In 1984, my lifelong buddy, Ted Craig, and I would run across the bridge as they replaced the roadway. The pictures show the way the bridge developed an arch in the roadway, because of the lighter road materials.

Flat before:

Slight arch after:

Porter:

In 1987, on the Bridge's 50th anniversary I was with the multitudes that caused the bridge to 'sigh', by flattening the road surface. Then on my 50th birthday my dear friend and mentor Bob Skutch gave me a piece of the original stainless-steel cables that were replaced and cut to 4-inch pieces and sold to the public as mementos.

In 1938, they started painting the bridge from one end to the other and when they were finished, they would start all over again. They did that for 66 years. In 2003 they stopped painting the bridge and it started to get rusty, corroded, dirty and ugly. I watched with horror. How could they treat "her" that way?

In 2018, I enrolled Lee Spellman and Greg Erker to help put together the Foundation, [TGGBBF]. We are looking for a major funder to complete the Foundation. We will succeed!

4-**Delancey City**:

Delancey City is based on changing our prison system, much like Finland and the Nordic countries have done. They did away with their prisons and have communities for rehabilitation.

 In 2019 I met three people from Finland, and they told me about the successful transition away from prisons like the dungeons of our present prison systems.

I went to the funeral of the Vice President of Delancey Street in San Francisco. My Friend John Harrison was a friend of the Founder Mimi Siebert. I wanted him to introduce me to her, which he did. While I was there, I saw; [Willie Brown ex-mayor of San Francisco, my tutor at Hastings law school and my lawyer], and almost a thousand graduates of the Delancey Street program.

I was impressed with their rehabilitation, dress, politeness, and camaraderie. I asked them what was the secret of Delancey Street program? What they told me was classic: They were learning to be responsible and accountable for their actions. They would make amends where needed for damage they had done to family and friends in the past. Now many of them were out in the world performing "miracles for change".

I was impressed. I asked them about the possibility of putting together a city that used the same concepts and training and make it an alternative to prisons. They asked me how you could do such a herculean task? I said all we have to do is imagine it and start following the energy. I said, if "Bugsy" Siegel could envision Las Vegas in the sands of Nevada, then we could envision the City of Delancey.

It would be a place of healing, with no barbed wire fences, no guards. The candidates or students [not criminals] would be able to bring their families, rent or own a home. It would be a regular city with schools, a library, a city hall, hospitals, parks, churches, and all the amenities of a modern city.

Here is how it would work: you are convicted in our present court system. You stand before the judge and he gives you a choice to go to one of our prisons like San Quentin or to Delancey City. For incorrigible convicts, we will modify the program. We want to change the existing system of retribution and punishment. Many criminals are not dangerous.

We need to look at the way we treat the average person and the way we treat the wealthy. This discrepancy in our legal system and how we handle crime causes a major problem in our society. It causes resentment, for the average person, and hypocrisy in the wealthy. It is not a fair system and it undermines our belief in a free democratic society. We will change this!

5-**The HOPEprogram**:

The HOPEprogram will assist teachers in purchasing a home in the community near their school. It will help them with their down payment, so they can afford to buy in any community. The Program is an entity of Pacific Rim Group and is projected to start in San Francisco, California. For more information check the website:
 portdavis.wixsite.com/thehopeprogram

The idea of The HOPEprogram, came to me in 1960. I was in law school. We were expecting our third child. We would need more space. I thought it would be better to buy now while prices are lower, and it would be a good investment for the future. To do this, we needed the down payment of 20 percent. We were able to borrow it from family.

The original price of $26,000, turned into a great investment as it sold in 2018 for $1,800,000.

The HOPEprogram will raise funds through the sale of stock, and the investors will share in the appreciation of the homes as the stock increases in value. The teachers will also get a percentage of the appreciation.

The benefits of this Program will reverberate throughout the community. The teachers will save time. They will not have to commute the many hours they spend driving to and from their homes in affordable communities. They will be able to walk to work and in many cases be able to sell a second automobile, reducing maintenance and commuting costs   It will reduce the stress of commuting. It will reduce the health dangers associated with living under constant stress. And more importantly it will allow them to have more after school time for their students and other school activities. This will allow them to have more time for their personal life and their families.

The students benefit by having access to the teacher whenever needed and the teacher will be more relaxed. The student's parents benefit as their children get better instruction from teachers, relieving the parents of having to tutor their children.

Therefore, the whole community will benefit as the schooling process becomes localized. This becomes a "WOW" moment for everyone and The HOPEprogram can bring this about. [Many of the concepts mentioned here were derived from Hillary Clinton's Book; IT TAKES A VILLAGE].

6- **Right to Die:**

This is one of the basic "Human Rights". I do not want anyone to tell me how I can or cannot die. I have talked to hundreds of friends and many acquaintances about their thought on the subject. I find that most people who are willing to talk about their death do not want government, the church, or the medical profession to dictate how or when one can die. We need to correct our thinking on this subject and remove any legislation that infringes on this basic human freedom.

In 2018 my sister was 88 years and had slowly lost her ability to care for herself. She was in a home with 5 other elders who were having the same problem.

Then she got sick, and to relieve her pain, the doctors administered morphine, but she was unable to eat or drink, and went into a coma. The nurse at the time told me that she would die in 5 days without food or water. When I saw her the last day of her life, she was like a vegetable and I thought that this morphine treatment was like a form of torture. Not only for my sister, but for all the people around her, especially her daughter who was with her every day.

I thought that it would have been more humane to allow my sister to take a pill and die instantly. We need to establish that we have a "right to die".

7- **Lifetime Education:**

If there is a secret in this lifetime, it is a lifetime of education, another "Human Right". When I grew up in Alameda, California, my parents sent me and my siblings to local schools. I was not a good student, but I did learn some basics. My parents always asked us how we did in school. What they looked for was our "grades". I thought "grades" were important. I did not think that "learning" was important. Yea; I had to know something to get a "grade". So. I would memorize what I thought I needed to get that all important "grade".

It was not until after my first marriage that I learned from the wonderful women in my life that it was "learning" that was important. "Learning" became important to me when I was in my 50's. Then I started to look at life differently. I would be interested in what I could "learn". So, I took programs for seniors, graduate courses, and workshops. A new world opened for me.

Gary Arnstein, a client of our mortgage company, invited us to a presentation about a Foundation, "Books for Nepal". We were going to a movie that night, and we could not say no to Gary, so my wife Maritza, and I agreed to attend. We decided to make our presence known, and then slip out the back door and go to our movie.

Well, that little "cloak and dagger " changed my life forever. When the Founder of "Books for Nepal", John Wood, started to make the presentation, which was the perfect time to "sneak" out the back door, Maritza said, "why don't we see what it is about first"?

The founder was one of the millionaires from Microsoft who had traveled through Nepal on a vacation. He was enthralled with the little kids because they seemed so friendly. They wanted his paperback books and anything that was in writing. He said that it affected him deeply and he had to do something about it. After he got home, he started sending books to his contacts in Nepal.

The people in Nepal were so grateful, that it made a powerful impression on him, and he had to return to Nepal to see what it was all about. When he got back to Nepal some of the kids from his first visit would greet him and thank him for his generosity.

Then, he met with the elders who were also very thankful. They showed him their troubles with education. They had few schools. They only sent young boys to the distant schools if they could afford it. Little girls were not offered the opportunity to go to school.

John quit Microsoft and changed the name of the Foundation to "Room to Read" which has become a worldwide foundation helping more than 16 million kids in 16 countries get an education. His books tell his personal story and how he did it.

Today you can send a little girl to school for a year by donating $250. You can build a library or a school for $3,000 with volunteer labor.

We never got to the movie. I do not even remember what it was. But I do remember that meeting in Mill Valley California.

We donated $250 before we left that night. And we made a commitment to donate $3,000 from our next jumbo loan. This was a no brainer.

Here is how we would do it:

1 - We would make a commission of $5,000 on a jumbo loan of $500,000 and donate $1,500 of our commission to the school.
2 - Our client would borrow $501,500 and donate $1,500 of it to the school.
3 – That is how we get the $3,000.
4 - The client would get a $1,500 tax deduction saving $800 in taxes.
5 - Thus, it only costs the client $700 which he borrowed.
6 – The extra $1,500 on the client's loan would increase the monthly payments less than $10. and some of that is a tax write off.

Now you can see why it is a "NO BRAINER"! The client can help build a school for 100 kids, for less than $10 a month.

This is not a hard sale. When you think of building a school for 100 kids for $10 a month, every one of my clients would do that.

We left the meeting on a high, and as we entered our car, Maritza suggested that we set up an organization like what Wood is doing. I was flabbergasted, "what are you talking about"? She said that we could set up a Foundation like "Books for Nepal" and do it for little girls in Peru [Maritza was born in Peru and came to the United States in 1970]. I said let's talk about it.

We did and we started "The Davis Foundation For Education" (TDFFE) especially for little girls in third world countries, starting with Peru. We presented the idea to her brothers and sisters in Peru and they decided to set up The Juan Arbocco Foundation For Education a sister foundation to The Davis Foundation For Education.

[I will donate all my profits from my speaking tour "We the People" XXI, to The Davis Foundation for Education].

Oh yea! Lifetime Education. I want to set up an organization that will put the pieces together so that we incorporate "free schooling" in the United States from birth to death. The benefits outweigh the initial costs. Because the more we are educated, the more we build a better society, the more we produce, and our gross domestic product will be astronomical. Another "WIN, WIN, WIN" IDEA.

[See "It Takes a Village" by Hillary Rodham Clinton]

8- Red Carpet Immigration:

Immigrants built this country, and this is one of the most important "Human Rights". We need to honor them by opening our doors to new immigrants. Basically, we all descended from immigrants. The way to a better and stronger society in the United States is to keep doing what worked for more than 500 years. Many of the original settlers had all kinds of backgrounds. Some were young, single, married with babies, professional, educated, and uneducated, and some with criminal records of all types.

They came with the promise of a new and better life. They went through a growth process over these hundreds of years, and we are the recipients of their work and struggles.

We should set up an immigration system that looks like a Red Carpet. It invites all, yes, even the so called criminals. Because that is what builds a strong and better society.

Ah! For those who are afraid we will protect you. Someone with a tainted record will be given a system of making amends.

We will have new arrivals sign in, get a registration number [eventually it becomes their Social Security Number], also take their DNA, fingerprints, voice, and eye prints. Then they will be offered jobs by all the businesses located right there, for convenience, that have signed up to hire them on for a period of 6 months, after which time they will report back on their progress and then be given an extension. Any illegal immigrant will no longer be called illegal. They will be called "UNREGISTERED" or "global citizen" and will then have to go through the immigration process.

The basic idea is to think in global, and inclusionary terms. When we think this way, we start to see our oneness. The earth is our sandbox, we can share it, or we can hoard it. We have the choice to be our better selves.

9-**The Electric Challenge**

1-The removal of the Electoral College.

The Electoral College is an "albatross" around our necks. It does not represent a free Democratic Government, as a candidate for President can obtain a minority of the popular vote and still win the election by obtaining enough electoral college votes to win. We have seen this in the last 16 years in the Bush vs Gore vote in 2000, and the Trump vs Clinton vote in 2016.

It has a psychological effect on the people in a very subtle and dangerous way. It really makes the candidates focus on only a few "Battle ground States" and this has a subconscious effect on all of us, as it does not represent what a true Democracy should be; a government; "of the people, by the people, and for the people". Obviously, many of us feel this delusion without talking about it.

2-<u>Electronic Voting</u>.

Voting is the most important "Human Right" to be established on a Federal level. We are in the age of technology. We can do everything electronically. We can bank, pay bills, store private information, email, and much more. China has a city that will not accept money, only a smart phone with electronic payments. Our grandparents now have "simple" smart phones, so they can keep in touch with their children and grandchildren, sending and receiving pictures and personal accomplishments.

The Voyager 1 and 2 missions launched into space in the 1970's, have sent back data for almost 40 years and they are light years into the universe, having sent close up images and scientific data from Jupiter, Saturn, Uranus and Neptune.

[this is mind boggling for many of us].

[Please *Google*:
*Technology Ideas, "E-Voting is a moonshot the U.S.
must take"; by Leonid Bershidsky November 7, 2020,
5:00AM PST.*
*https://www.bloomberg.com/opinion/articles/2020-
11-07/election-2020-results-make-e-voting-a-must-do-
moonshot-for-the-u-s*

*Imagine that you could vote securely on your
smartphone, change your vote any time before Election
Day, and know that your vote has been counted.*

*The crazy quilt Americans call their election process has
produced another nail-biter in 2020, with delays caused
by everything from postal bottlenecks and voting
machine <u>malfunctions</u> to an unexpected <u>shortage of
printer ink</u>. The way votes are collected and counted in
the U.S. makes recounts, lawsuits and sometimes
lingering doubts over an election's true outcome all but
inevitable: You don't have to be Donald Trump to
worry that errors could have tilted a tight count toward
the opposing side. There could be an APP for that.
There is a 21st-century cure for these ills.*]

I have contacted an "AI" [Artificial
Intelligence] company that says they have the
system for Electronic Voting [EV] that is full
proof and cannot be hacked or tampered with.

Ever since the first election in 1788, there have been many methods used to disenfranchise the people. We saw this in our recent 2020 election. There are too many incidents that have been used to deny many of us our right to vote. None of this will occur in an EV system.

In 2014 Dave Schwartz and I were discussing the 2000 election and the ruling of the United States Supreme Court. In that ruling, the Court overruled the Supreme Court of Florida, which had ruled that the Florida Counties should all use the same method in counting the votes of the "Hanging Chads". As the Counties completed their new method of counting, Gore kept getting many more votes, and it was predicted that had all the counties completed their counting, Gore would have won by hundreds if not thousands of votes. Because the vote counting was stopped, Gore lost by 537 votes, but he won the popular vote nationwide.

U. S. Supreme Court Justice Sandra Day O'Connor was the 5th and deciding vote stopping the counting in Florida. After she retired from the Court, she said it was a mistake and the Supreme Court should not have taken the case. And Gore probably would have become President.

No wonder people do not trust the system. That is another reason <u>to re-ordain</u> and <u>re-establish</u> the Constitution in the twenty-first century.

What I am interested in achieving is to bring Democracy to all the people. Obviously, our present system is not Democracy in its true definition. As Dave and I continued to brainstorm the effect of that Supreme Court decision, we started to look at "who is able to vote", and "why is it important"?

In a Democracy the "power" is the vote of the people. First, we said that everyone should be able to vote. The reason it is important is that everyone wants to feel included. Especially if they take the Preamble to the Constitution literally; "We the People". Most people I talk to say that "We the People" includes them, and everyone else. Dave and I agree.

So, who is everyone else?

In 1872 the Suffragette Susan B. Anthony voted and was arrested and fined over $100 [a value over $2,000 in 2020]. She was not forced to pay the fine and was released from jail. [President Donald Trump Pardoned her in 2020]

Susan said that the Preamble included all the people in the United States as well as the equal protection clause of the 14th Amendment, and that she was a person and therefor apart of the people and she should be able to vote.

So, who is everyone else?

Then we had a long discussion about who "we" are? The hot tub was too hot, and we took a break. We met later and continued our brainstorm. We said that too many people were being left out and we started to include everyone that has a stake in our government. This was a lot of fun. We decided to set a certain criterion and include everyone who is:

> 1-A natural born citizen.
>
> 2-Obtain a social security number online.
>
> 3-Be a resident for 5 years.
>
> 4-Pay taxes to IRS for at least 2 years.
>
> 5-Pass a test on the constitution in English.
>
> 6-Be a Mother
>
> 7-All felons
>
> 8- If all these criteria are met, then they can register to vote, online.

+1- Bill of "Human Rights"

We will create a Bill of Human Rights and add them to the United States Constitution:

1-Right to Immigrate.

2-Right to Vote.

3-Right to Health Care

4-Right to Education

5-Right to Die.

6-Right to Abortion

7-Right to Housing

8-Right to Income

3. 17th and 18th Century Thinking

The thinking of the Colonists was directly related to the European politics, philosophy, and science of the times. Communications were radically reoriented during the course of the "long 18th century" (1685-1815). It was part of a movement referred to by its participants as the Age of Reason, or simply the Enlightenment.

The Enlightenment thinkers in Britain, France and throughout Europe questioned traditional authority and embraced the notion that humanity could be improved through rational change. The Enlightenment produced numerous books, essays, inventions, scientific discoveries, laws, wars and revolutions.

The American and French Revolutions were directly inspired by the Enlightenment ideals.

The American Colonists had left the Old World to find new adventures and a better life. They were adventurous and had to come up with how to live in a new society. The King wanted to rule them by the standards and methods that were prevalent in England. But these were not popular with the Colonists.

There was a need to develop a better way to live. Also, a better way to govern. As the difference in these ideas, between the King and the Colonists, became apparent, it caused many problems that led up to the American Revolution and the Declaration of Independence, which detailed their grievances.

The Colonists became revolutionaries, and when they won the war, they had to decide how to Govern themselves. First, they established the Articles of Confederation and then the Constitution. This took several years, and in 1787 they completed the Constitution.

That was the way the Founding Fathers were taught to think. They were the more educated. They were the ones who wanted to be part of the new government. They were the present leaders in the Colonies and the fledgling States. They had the experience and financial ability to spend the time formulating the Continental Congress and the Constitutional Convention.

They chose who could vote. They had heated discussions about the new government and compromised on many issues. Especially the famous [or infamous] "Electoral College".

That was the way they thought in the 1700's. A precedent was established, and it continues to the present day.

It takes a lot of time to make changes to our Constitution, but the time has come to make those changes.

4. Democracy and Capitalism

Democracy in combination with Capitalism were responsible for the tremendous growth and power of the United States. They co-exist in some form of harmony.

Democracy was a new concept of self-government. It was supposed to be a government; "of the people, by the people, and for the people". The power was to come from the people, by their vote.

[NOTE: ALL THE METHODS THAT HAVE BEEN USED FOR 233 YEARS TO LIMIT OR DENY THAT RIGHT, TO VOTE]

It was an experiment by the Founding Fathers that would preserve individual rights, State rights and guarantee a central government that would be run by elected officials voted on every 2 ,4, and 6 years, by the PEOPLE.

Capitalism was an economic and political system in which a country's trade and industry are controlled by private owners for profit, rather than by the government.

5. Power   [The Right to Vote]

The Power in a Democracy is supposed to be derived from the People by a Right to Vote, another "Human Right". It was a great idea. The People vote for representatives who serve at the will of the people. But this is not how it worked in the United States for 233 years.

[NOTE: ALL THE METHODS THAT HAVE BEEN USED FOR 233 YEARS TO LIMIT OR DENY THAT RIGHT, TO VOTE]

1787 thinking allowed for only 6% of the population to control the power, as they were the only ones with the right to vote. This group has held onto that power for 233 years.

In order to get the power back to the people, we will have to use twenty first century thinking. We will use the technology of the 2020's. The first place we use it is the right to vote. Then we establish who are the people who can vote, and we change that to include all residents, not just U. S. Citizens.

We adopt Electronic Voting. We allow people to register online. We allow people to vote online. We take a census online. We create an "APP" online, called "We the People" XXI, for the people to use to get a real consensus of what the people want. **NOTE: The APP is expected in the not too distant future.**

We need to include all the people; it will create a national healing. We need to change the way we think about each other and we need to include everyone. How can we do that? We need to change the way we think about citizenship. Where did citizenship come from and why did it exclude so many people?

Citizenship was a term used in the states of ancient Greece. Its meaning has changed over the centuries. We want to have another term used for people who are not natural born Citizens but are contributors to the society and the government of the United States. [See above ideas from Porter and Dave Schwartz in 2014].

Maybe we can expand the concept of citizenship to include all people residing in the United States as "Global Citizens" and include them in the original 6%. That means no matter how you got into the United States you are a "Global Citizen" and have certain rights, mainly the right to vote.

If anyone wants to be part of our society and have the right to vote, we will set up a new system for them:

1-A natural born citizen.

2-Obtain a social security number online.

3-Be a resident for 5 years.

4-Pay taxes to IRS for at least 2 years.

5-Pass a test on the constitution in English.

6-Be a Mother

7-All felons

8- If all these criteria are met, then they can register to vote, online.

When entering the United States, Companies will have jobs available and there will be a period of probation [6 months] and then an application for permanent residency. This will be called "Red Carpet" immigration.

As you read this, notice how you react to these proposals.

Under this system immigrants will feel like an invited guest. They will have an opportunity to have a voice, in a much simpler Democratic system. It might become easier to get to vote by starting a family and becoming a part of the community. We need to expand our thinking.

6. 21st Century Thinking

We are in the 21st century and times have changed. We know that there is more involved in people's behavior. We have learned so much about how we humans learn, grow, and develop our emotional, psychological, and spiritual awareness. We are able to deal with people's fears, pain, anger, and loss. This knowledge will allow us to change our laws.

We should look at where the thinking of legal and regulatory systems came from. People were hurt by someone and in order to feel better they wanted to blame them, punish them, and get retribution. It was a way to remove the pain. But it created separation and was only a band aid; it was fear-based thinking.

We will look at the way criminal laws are set up and how the wealthy are able to have a different system of how laws are implemented. Once we find out what that is about, we can make a fair system for all.

Finland did away with their prisons, and capital punishment. It is a leader in the 21st century, along with Norway and Sweden, on how we can handle crime or inappropriate behavior.. Their experience shows us how we can help people correct their behavior.

What if we really put our efforts into the Homeless issues, so we can start to find the solutions? Or, that health care comes before Aircraft Carriers? What if we stop policing the world and let the United Nations do it? I do not want to say we should not have a great military, but keep it focused on defense. More importantly, support the UN in doing the policing.

We need to study the way a society protects its members from being harmed by others. Policing is an important part of it, but is there a better way? Should we come up with another name for it? I watch the way our police become militant. I do not think that is the answer. We need to find a way to have local protectors in small communities, like the village concept of the past.

When I see police chasing violators in cars and the damage done to innocent bystanders, in an effort to catch someone, it seems irrational. Maybe we should let them go and use technology to find them. Our whole system of laws and methods of protecting each other needs to be re-thought using 2020 thinking. Again, the year of "clear Vision". We are lucky to be alive. We have the ability to research and change how we live with each other.

7. Inclusive vs Exclusive

My purpose in writing this book is to expose "exclusionary thinking" and create a society of "inclusionary thinking".

 I have expressed this in other chapters of the book as well. I want to advocate the principle that everyone should be included and have a voice in choosing what kind of a society we want to be. This includes ALL people, including our youth [with no age limits].

Our Founding Fathers were white men over 21 who owned property. Everyone else was left out. That club still exists today. The concept of exclusion is a belief system that many people support. There is something in the human psyche that comes from some kind a knee jerk reaction, that this is my turf, or my way of thinking and I am right, and you have no right to be here or to think the way you do..

 The Kumpuris Family Distinguished Lecture Series event in **S**eptember 2019, Honored Justice of the U.S. Supreme Court Ruth Bader Ginsburg. Bill Clinton introduced the ***justice***. The event was sponsored by the ***Clinton Foundation***, and her topic was: " We the People."

She talked about the Exclusion of so many people in the formation of the Country in 1787. Then she talked about how it took 233 years to Include more of us, and the need to Include everyone in the future.

8 "APP" - "We the People" XXI

How do we incorporate the ideas of the 21st Century? Electronically!

We can put together an "APP", call it "We the People" XXI, and let everyone living in the United States join it. We will have rules for participation. The idea is to find Social Causes that all people agree are needed for a better society. This will not be related to a particular political party.

We will have it go viral across the country and get 300,000,000 people, or more, using it. Then we can have discussions online about our Concerns and Causes.

 We honor the people who are willing to march in the streets for important Causes. There are many of us who do not march in the streets, but who support those that do, and the ideas they are promoting. There is another way for us non-marchers to participate. We can do it on the "We the People" XXI "APP".

Once we have reached a consensus; we will vote for candidates who espouse our new thinking. I call this 21st Century thinking.

I Learn so much from the youth of our country. They will be able to freely express their point of view. There is no age limit for using the "We the People" XXI "APP" - only passing a test based on the rules.

In 2018, after the shooting at the Florida high school, when the students got on National television and shared their concerns and ideas about gun control, I was impressed. They were 14, 16, 18 years old and were more eloquent than any politician I heard speak on the subject. When people on the "APP" come up with a consensus like the students, then our representatives can act on our behalf.

Some of these Social Causes will be so important that we will call them "Human Rights".

I propose that we develop a new "Bill of Human Rights", like the 1st 10 amendments to the United States Constitution and make them the next amendments

Oh! What fun we will have in the 21st Century, updating the United States Constitution, with 300,000,000 people being involved. This will demonstrate the power of Democracy, in action, including all the people to re-ordain and re- establish this Constitution for the United States of America.

This will demonstrate the essence of "INCLUDING" everyone, as Justice Ruth Bader Ginsburg suggested in 2019, and Dean Erwin Chemerinsky, Dean of the University of California Law School at Berkeley, California in his book titled; We the People, printed in 2018.

That will be a "WOW" moment in our history.

[FOR THE UNITED STATES OF AMERICA]

9- Who Are "We"?
Who aren't "We"?
and
Why is it Important?

Preamble to the
United States Constitution;

"We the people of the United States in order to form a more perfect union, establish justice, ensure domestic tranquility, provide for the common defense, promote the general welfare, and secure the blessings of liberty to ourselves and our posterity, do ordain and establish this Constitution for the United States of America."

This Preamble, as set forth by Gouverneur Morris, is the foundation from which we will build a "MORE PERFECT UNION" in the twenty-first century.

We will include everyone.
We will re-write how we vote, who can vote, and make sure our elected representatives are responsive to us, and not to an elitist financial group.

How "We the People" XXI evolved
My "Mind Map"

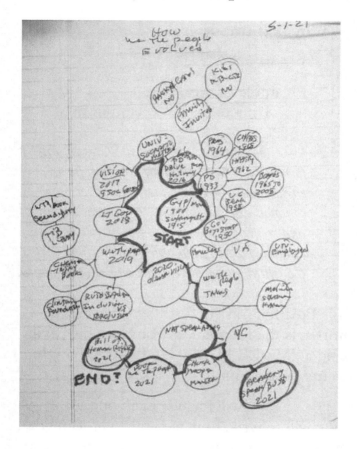

My Inspiration

2020
YEAR OF "CLEAR VISION"

2020 was a year of growth. I will tell you how it happened.

In 2017-19 I decided to work on 9 Social Causes, as I was doing this, Vicki Luisi suggested that I get a more stable income and I started driving for UBER In 2019.

I was driving for UBER in 2020. Also, I was starting a speaking tour on the Preamble to the United States constitution. The title to my speeches is: "WE THE PEOPLE". I did 8 speeches before March 2020, and then the Pandemic hit.

I had to stop driving for Uber and stop doing speeches. I ran out of money and lost my apartment-share. I only had Social Security income. I became homeless and my friend Jim Daley set up a temporary room for a week. Then I lived in my car for another week. My daughter Courtenay suggested that I call Marin Services, and they provided a motel room, where I stayed for 4 months.

While I was there, social distancing, I had my computer and was able to work. I searched for speaking opportunities, and found Ted's and National Speakers Association, so I joined the National Speakers Association and registered with Ted's.

Then I contacted the Veterans Administration, about some abscessed teeth and rental support. They decided to pay for an apartment. I found my present home at 1300 Lincoln Village Circle #257, but they would not do my teeth.
I had lost all my furniture after the 2008 Great Recession and needed to acquire more. So, I went on NEXT DOOR and found 70 pieces free.

I had 150 boxes and pictures in storage and with the new furniture and furnishings I have an exquisite home that looks like someone spent $10,000 to do it.

I had taken the California State Bar Exam 4 times 60 years ago and decided to take it the 5th time. I registered, joined a Bar review course, and studied 20 hours a week for 4 months, and 2 weeks before the Bar Exam in October, the California State Bar notified me that I was ineligible. I am appealing their decision.

My college sweetheart, Shannon who lives in Hawaii, had recently been widowed and I started calling her in March as a support. All her family live on the Mainland USA. We have talked every day for a year. I found out that I never lost that love I had for her 70 years ago. We would talk for an hour and it seemed like 5 minutes.

After I joined the Northern California Speakers Association, the director asked me what I talked about? I told him the Preamble to the United States Constitution, and my speeches are about "We the People". He said I want to mentor you. You will be able to start a speaking business and charge from $1,000 to $10,000 per talk, depending on how good you are.

We have met twice, and I joined their Speakers Academy course which helps one develop a successful business. One day he asked me for my speech outline and when he saw it, he said I should write a book about it. It took me two months, and I completed it on March 3, 2021. It is now being edited for publication.

I contacted my 3rd wife Karen Cowell during this period and as we talked, I realized she was the perfect one to get the funding we needed for The HOPEprogram. Initially she was reticent, but I told her she didn't have to sell it. All she had to do was support me in getting appointments with major companies who would want to do our startup funding. When she realized what I was seeking from her, she said OK, but you have to put together a 5-minute speech about it. I was delighted and am in the process of doing it.

Now you know why I had a great year and I call it the year of "Clear Vision" 2020

My Very Best,
Porter

FINAL THOUGHT

Who are we?
Who aren't we?
and
Why is it important?

Because: we will RE-ORDAIN and
RE-ESTABLISH the United States
Constitution for the United States of America,
using **twenty-first century thinking**
and adopting a **"Bill of Human Rights"**.

[If the Founding Fathers could update society,
form a Democratic government, and take the
power away from the King, his Parliament, his
Army, his Navy, and his Governors, then we
can do it in a peaceful way, using,
twenty first century thinking and
technology].

There is a famous saying:

**"If you believe it won't happen,
you won't see it when it does."**

THINK

INVITE: Porter to Speak at your event

CURRENT TOPICS: include

15-20 minutes "We the People" XXI
Thought provoking lunchtime talk.

15-20 minutes "We the People" XXI
Raising awareness – Pol Sci Class

30-60 minutes "We the People" XXI
Law School - Get the juices rolling

30-60 minutes "We the People" XXI
"Conversation, Cookies & Coffee";
Informal setting lots of give and take.

15 to 60 minutes "The HOPEprogram"
Home program for Teachers

■■■

EMAIL: porter@porterspeaks.com

WEB-SITE: www.porterspeaks.com

Thank you for reading!

Made in the USA
Middletown, DE
08 May 2022

65437770R00046